Elephant Moon
Songs & Poems

by Jade Alger

ISBN-13: 978-0692532287
ISBN-10: 0692532285

Cover design, typesetting and illustrations by Jade Alger
Typeset in Adobe Caslon Pro, 11pt
Published by Picturedrome Palace Books®

Contents

To Janka, Princess Tia & dear friend, Aimee Riley

Author's Prologue

The following poems, songs and scribbles came to life over a period of about five years, with a few of the songs from an earlier time. The selected works are of course, only a handful from many dusty journals that sit in my nightstand and as with everything, it is difficult to choose those which carry the most sway. I've found most of my inspiration in time spent in Slovakia with my wife Janka and travels to other magical lands, the latest being Kauai, Hawaii. Oftentimes it only takes a peculiar ray of moonlight combined with a strong imagination to carry my pen across paper in a way that I hope will reawaken lost dreams in all who dare to dream. Most of all, God's Spirit quickens my thoughts to the mysteries that abound. So to all travelers, magicians, artisans, minstrels and dreamers, these pages are for you.

Musings of Jasper Fox

Her shadow mixes with the moon
In my porcelain teacup
Spinning with the whipped liqueur
A barmy blend of sweet light
Washing the tip of my spoon

Bounces off these walls, her voice
Encumbered by nothing
Loved by few
Yet prized and preserved in my memory

Sweltering tears roll around and around
and down and down
To a place where accordion people play
and chat over coffee at the Night Café

Where Agnieszka sadly counts the hours
Tapping her heels to the Waltz of the Flowers

I approach the catwalk
Overcome by Foxglove and Creeping Jenny
These blossoms scream color
And smile as I pass
They bow

The bells of St. Michael's remind me
Brass echoes across the farthest hilltops
Resounding
Upon the flavored season

Like swathes of flashback reflections dim
I see things that have been put away for years
In the dusty drawer
Under papers
Suddenly her eyes jolt my brain
Stopped coldly in my tracks

My fingers curl
Twisting thoughts find one second of relief
And glide to safety

Now a carousel breeze from the mechanical fair
Swings through my shirt and then through my
hair

Sweltering tears roll around and around
and down and down
To a place where accordion people play
and chat over coffee at the Night Café

Where Agnieszka sadly counts the hours
Tapping her heels to the Waltz of the Flowers

Her apron sweeps across my arm
I tug at her
Dangling fabrics
Imploring that she take a seat
Let's speak of love, respect, life
Of death

Share your truths
If you don't know how to speak I'll watch
Your fingers dance across the keys
Share your muse
Any revelation? Any at all?
I want to revel in your sing-song rhythm
Those festive arts
You hide

Deep
    Dark whispers
Soak the back of my neck
What is it?
Who's there?
Ah, but that she would just once more appear

I would paint her portrait permanent
Inside
And meditate on what I've lost

At once a tune cuts through the fog
A minstrel show at Orchard Knob

Sweltering tears roll around and around
and down and down
To a place where accordion people play
and chat over coffee at the Night Café

Where Agnieszka sadly counts the hours
Tapping her heels to the Waltz of the Flowers

Electrify the Rooftops

There is lightning in the room tonight
A scent of unobscured love
We welcome a unified Presence
And shake the invisible hand

There's a luster in my affection this night
A tug beneath my chair
Ancient hearts melt into children
Engrossed in a love affair

Delicately quilted are the heavens
Descending into our hands
Unburdened and weightless we wait
In our calmly spinning stance

There is lightning in the room tonight
Heaven's breath has turned to speak
Verbalize your gracious intentions
Let me shake your invisible hand

Pearl of Považie

O Trenčín Fair
Lord of the Váh
Pillar of Great Moravia
Adorned in white
Your hillsides roll
Through woodlands deep
And halls of stone

Fatima's veil,
Your legends keep
Locked away in time
Under beechen leaves

He sought her hand
In nightshade glen
Under frozen cliffs
And taverns dim

Forged a fountain rich
Mlynská belfry climbs
To free her heart
Immortal yearnings tied

Robed in prowess true
He tarried nevermore
A quest to prove his love
Omar, a chasm bore

She stood in amber night
Withdrew her shadowed hair
It fell in ebony folds
Unwatched on pathways bare

Starless waters calm
A princess soul still sleeps
Through unseen doors
Medieval voices speak

O Trenčín Fair
City of dreams
Your ghostly profile stands
Etched in eternity

Of Peregrine Visitations and Light

Beside a paint-chipped window
With a face still imprinted by pillow patterns
Faint pin strokes of morning sun stream in

Dressed hurriedly in my snug cap and breeches
Naked toes shocked by cold floorboards
I inadvertently turn toward the glass

To my wonderment, a winged raptor
Alights; transfixed in time. Feelings grow
Throbbing sensation — See! A spectral friend
It's the electrifying dazzler!

It is then, in that sweet moment that
Murky minutes come to a punctual halt
The silhouetted adumbration —
Hooked beak and sharp eyes; my visitor

And just as easy as He came
In His stealth feathered coat,
As if with the tip of His hat,
Gigantic wings unfold and He dips his neck

Lets go the offshoot and floats on air
Through a criss-cross puzzle of trees
Obscurely divine, this esoteric missile of prey
Gyrfalcon, phantom messenger, plumed angel

At once it's over;
The bird has retreated to the living wood
Another prophetic manifestation ended
And as I pull my numb fingers from the ledge,
In the wind — the unearthly, piercing cry
of that unmistakable Falcon

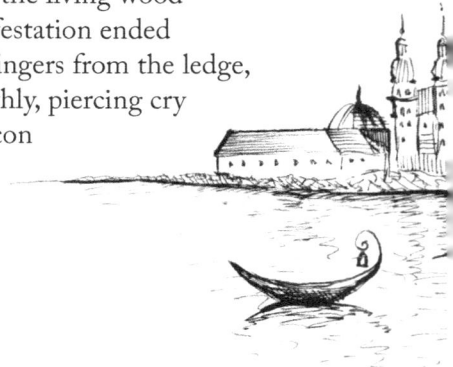

Anton's Daydream
(as scribbled from a boat)

When our circumstance looks bleak
And hasty winters make for achy joints

    Orion flickers her sky-hanging lanterns
    From her distant home
    To our rooms by the sea

As if to tell us of youth and vigor
And the pure merry-making of simple hearts

    The Elephant Moon hovers over the forest
    Anointing the treetops with her afterglow paint
    Two streets down from this haunted marina
    Tavern-strewn love notes and hat-feathered friends

When night's whispering veil has fallen
And our governing eyes no longer see

    Orion flickers her sky-hanging lanterns
    From her distant home
    To our rooms by the sea

And I hope that the Elephant Moon,
that the Elephant Moon comes to visit me

Catacombs

Bewitched by the glare of the daredevil Moon
A dreamy night skates in through skeleton trees
Animating shadows — rearranging time
    And the clock face winks

Evening's lantern throws tiny flickers of light
Into the yawning bowels of an adventurous earth
The starry eyes of the lost boys spring open
    As the farcical drama ensues

Safe harbor for the restless
A misfit's lagoon
The free spirits' Wonderland;
    This zig-zag tomb

A labyrinthine circus
Descends through jingle-jangle halls
Where an ethereal music
Is breathing in the walls

Listen! An echo beneath the surface
A mob of madmen down below
Where the outcast finds her solace
Where the peculiar people go
    Nurtured in the seamlessness of night

As the World Turns

A complicated web of juniper leaves
Traps stars that flex o'er sleepless seas
And flicker down into our earthen womb
Making glitter the salty dew

Aimless configurations
Step with the rolling of the tide
The wavy personality of our rippled floor
Time-worn, heaving, undulating void
Our Reflective Riddler

Beachhut lampposts, those glowing ghosts
Signal the path of the purring coast
Where lover's footprints come and go
As the world turns

Memories Revisited

In that undecided hour before dawn
At the end of a disfigured street
Cello strings linger and play
In the dew-speckled mist

Droning ensues from the mouth of a hollow
A bright-eyed memory bank
Once music hall; now obscure souvenir shop
Starlit portal to a miniature world

I doff my silk hat and dangle my toes on the brickwork
Led irresistibly into the margins of time
Driven into the belly of the whale
Suspended by a tangy sense of wonder
Strapped in a theatrical chair

Gestural shadows sweep the ceiling
A kingly curtain rises up through the air
Behold—Spectacle des Enfants de France!

The stage is a kaleidoscope
Engagement for the eyes
Storytellers, wigmakers, scene-painters, costumiers
Pyrotechnicians, apparitions, invisible puppeteers
Optical illusions transform the night café
  As we slip behind the misty morning veil

To a place both unadulterated and unexplored

Ferris Wheel Tree

How pleasant doth that moon seem
When shaking in the waves
How delicate her eyelids
When startled by a dream
How faithfully she opens
When touched beneath the wings

How winsome are the fruit trees
When colored by the clouds
How quick to shed a teardrop
Her lashes spit them out
How angelic is Christmas
When miracles occur

I'm looking down from a Ferris Wheel Tree
Spooked by the lighthouse upon me stays
Sometimes at night I can hear her shadow
Move through the leaves under window-candles play

The fringes are pregnant with laughter sleepy
Wheels of life take us with hands unfurled
Up to the gates of the frothy mountains
Snow in our eyes and our britches torn

Juggernaut of Super-Shooting Beam

Clairvoyant we won't become
This side of the coffin
Patient hearts await the night
When we won't feel the razors

Lusting for the break of day
Craving social justice
The avenues of heaven stir
Abundant fields of rain

Somewhere in the aftermath
We won't be the same
By and by the doors unfold
To swooshing lands of gladness

All of my trinkets I believe
To tempt me to believe that
This world is all that I own

Semi-understanding's all I've got
I can never be arrayed like a
Juggernaut of Super-Shooting Beam

Somewhere when I die I'll reach the twist
I won't be ornery
I won't be a savage

I still eat the dirt by night
Feathers depict my love
Still I cannot fully grasp
The situations rising

A poof of air from heaven's atmosphere
Would be a soothing reminder
Life is running out of time
To make room so life may begin

Windows On Beckov

Secretly the fountain Kings
Slide beneath old castle wings
Lifting those latches,
   Laughing—

Christmas is almost here
The joy is everywhere

Hearts in love come swiftly on
Now we need your lucky charm
Candles in windows
   Alit with—

The Spirit of Christmas wine
Lost in snowy time

Twinkling ice beneath them sounds
Twirling in a circle round
Dance for us metal shoes
   Snug and warm—

Snowflakes fill the air
Long, dark Christmas hair

Somberly our shadows stretch
Toward the stones under the hedge
Overlapping the ivy tails
   Of the fountain Kings—

Leap through the wintry lights
The village is bound in white

God, I know you guide my steps
Boots with bells beneath me tread
Hasten me to my lover's door
She awaits my gifts—

Christmas is almost here
The joy is everywhere
Skating about on wheels
Tapping their Christmas heels
Spectator eyes are born
What comes with the morrow's morn

Secretly the fountain Kings
Slide beneath old castle wings
Lifting those latches,
    Laughing—

Christmas is almost here
The joy is everywhere

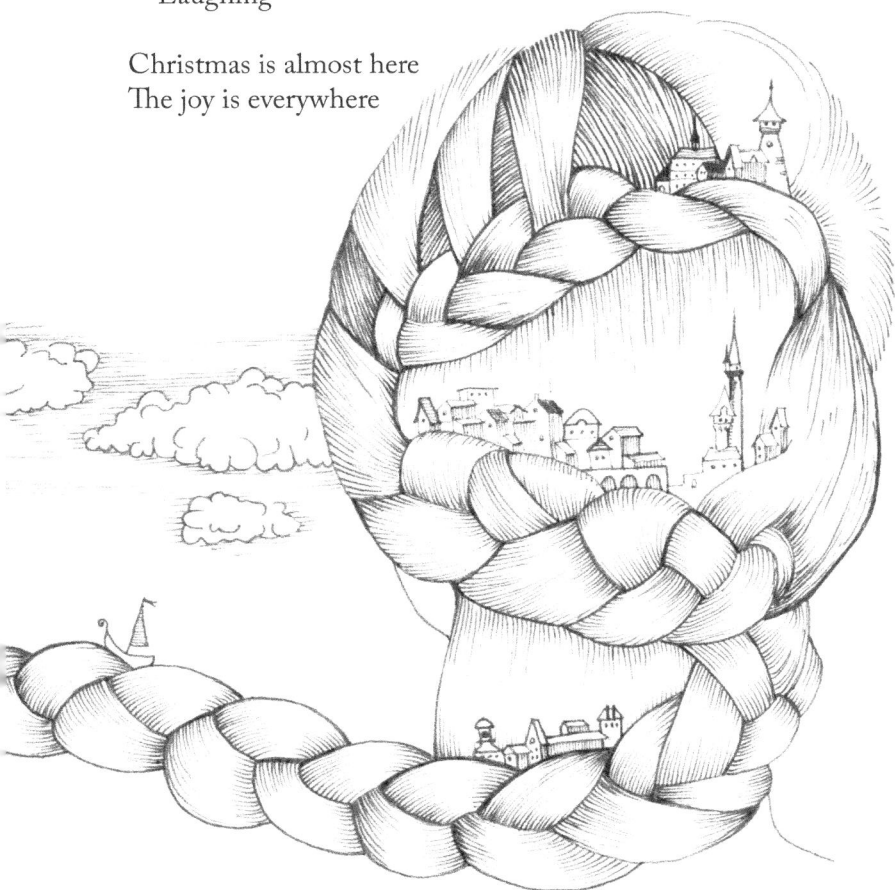

Carolina Belle

The dwarf apple maze
Is a seaman's greenlit haven
Clippership den
It's a seaside garden city
Flinging masts across its waters
Hollow spires wait for God
In the blanketed bosom caverns of the Carolina Belle

Saturated skies bleed with yellow lines of lightning
Pointed down through radiant rooftops, glazed faces
and sleeping sailors
Mobs of horse-drawn dames
Riffling through their crinkle-worn broadsheets
Beside the brink where ocean fingers
Reach cock-eyed cockleshells and jolly boats

Ahead on the byway
A zig-zag caricature princess
Feeds her gaslight match stick
To the droopy-hooked beacon

Sir Bimbley tilts a bony knee
Waves his handblown glass caddy
Asking a half-penny fortune
For cultivated sweetmeats and lustrous bonbon dainties

Now when a fire balloon on Quay Landing
Attracts frock-laden ladies
Through the fanlights of flip-flop dwellings or
    chateau-basted buildings
Spots the resplendent diorama

Onward three-dimensional figures
Cannon babes and twinkle starlings
Swiftly baked and breaded pudding
Scented within the yellow cultivar walls

The equestrian thruways
Bucklebent and bowlegged ponies canter
Twixt galleyfoist and the devilish deep
Dolphin dinghy dungeon

I in my Tam o'Shanter and frilled garments
Stand ignorant of background colors
Against a pale and scenic jungle
I juggle my own red-bellied footsteps

Amid a dreary penguin cave
Where the leviathan perches for respite
Covered in seaweed with fireflamed eyeholes
Ready to quilt the world asunder

Oh, one last glance at the steepled horizon
The sky needles that play with wispy armies of fog
Set solid and aimed to unfurl madly
With a faint touch from the spring-wound finback

Hoist my tongue to a topmost vertex
Animate my psyche with your frozen tarts
For all that sucks in air and stirs on the motionless surf
Is the very backbone of a maritime possibility

Toy figureheads mark the outer skyline
In my depths, an ear-popping echo
Sing to me windjammers, sharecroppers, and
    skirt-tootsied maidens
Let us launch our fresh fangled charge

Pattering past cobbled corners
Clusters of signal houses and sweetshops
Mounds of lengthwise pastry parlors
Under overhung balcony pouches

Encamped in the ivy, smothered in passion
I crave the theatre and covet the ocean

She falls through a net of lacework and textures
To open her labyrinthine puzzle

Dribbling cloudbursts spit and splutter
Sheets of sky drench the evening
Schooners meander porpoise waters
In this wharf-cleansed, diehard, whistle-stop city

Sketch your canvas memoir
On pages of sweetgrass, wafer-thin paper
Stage your Spinstep, trip-the-light shimmy
Feast and let go the reigns of the future

It's a cagelike rabbit-hole hamlet
Filled with reverberations and an itch to begin singing
Lift these streetdoors, peer down into earth's rib cage
Wherefrom spill the feelings we yearn to start kissing

Heartlessly drumming the rich orchard soil
Flailing the gate with hammertail fists
We are fighting to seize the untamed flash
And embrace these now starshingled spaces

Oh celestial stairways and galleries
Live on painting your designs in my tomb
My carcass shakes like an electrified madman
My songs rise above these enfeebled old boots

Sails, shapes and shanties
Here, my skeleton-scaffold chassis
Folds up tight in a seashell of pain
Bursts forward like a tidalwave surge

Beyond the deck hands and serpentine vessels
The planted dreams of a ship-sleeping river
Diving down to scoop up dismissed stories
From the voices rinsed away with the years

The obedient pulse of horse-hooved passages
Open-air vending and petite church-goers
A silhouetted suitcase fellow, embarrassed scandal trot
From the angled Museum Alley
To the lips of the incestuous pool

Laborious rooms above Boston Ivy balustrade
Permanent perennial hangings
Seem to support the fluctuating avenues
Whereupon youths go hoop rolling and Scotch-hoppers

Crosshatched ornaments are printed,
    scratched and stippled
Deliberately burned into my flesh
As I ease a wooden skiff across this puddle
Shimmering salt water and taffy-dazzled mesh

There's a wasteland in the briny deep of my own bosom
And its undulating wobble will not cease
When I stoop to catch the harness
    with hook-held feelers
An explosively loud whisper calms likely shadows

The lay of the acres;
The laughing serenity of the village reflections
Bring my ghost a human face
That surreal tint of a living and undying expression
A mask of certainty, a quick symbol of truth

Alas, trolley car villa
Illumines quake-infested gambrels
Near quiet assemblies of aged dimestore centers
Over a balcony-bathed kitchen where I linger

Huddled misshapen and bedazzled
I cower amid the flanking pelicans
Unwaveringly yielded to oncoming spasms
Of foundation earth when it throws fits and spits

I'm cupped to the rails overlooking this spectacle
Pulled like the workings of a timekeeping ticker
Click clock, the hands and the bells of quiet chaos
Hold a steady hum in my buttoned up absence

Rocks curl under hillside dale tables
When the clammy webs outstretched,
    reveal untold fables
From a sidestepped rhythm;
I'm part of a listless conversation
Yet I glow with uncluttered meaning

In the air is a song and my hands can't stop shaking
I'm the gift of the heavens as I lean
Deep the thirst for quenching this sting
I awake in a ship-yard night
Gazing through the clouds of time
        —at the depths of his eyes

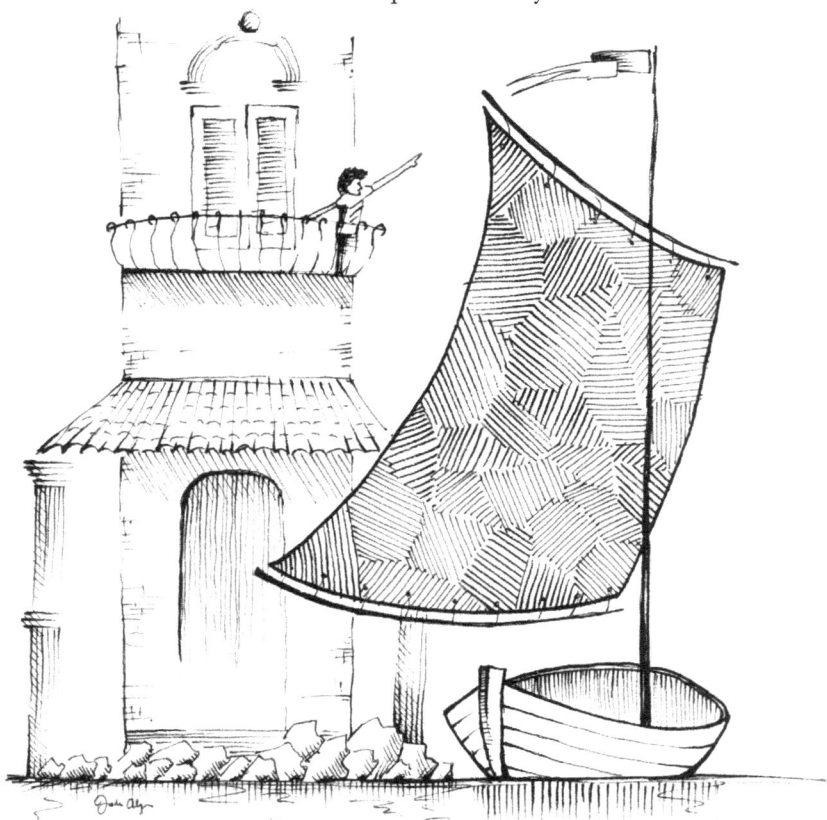

It's the penny-eyed nostalgia
Nibbling at my nose
Seduces with her long-worn dress
Then scuttles off over window ledge
Panting as she goes

———◆◆———

Leaves
Masters of Color
Remind us that prime moments
Come and Go
Quickly

———◆◆———

Footsteps
My own red-bellied
Standing ignorant of
The quilted background sky table
Stepping

———◆◆———

We gathered the dogs
And started across Alaska
The pink moon
Unfolding on the plain

———◆◆———

We aren't encamped on this earth
To harm souls
These sacred moments
Are fleeting treasures
When fully employed
Produce
Love

❖

It Happened at Piccadilly
A Page from my Waistcoat Pocket

Yesterday our shadows kissed on a fairground wall
Today I rehearse Jazz syncopation
Overlooking a web of city lights and Spa Island

The moon, locked in sky, begins her quiet revolt
She awaits her nightly performance from behind
    the celestial curtain
Then beguiles spectators with her eerie countenance
As she slides along her predetermined archway

Like interlocking latticework, piano notes huddle close
Then scatter like the fiery tails of a Fizzigig sky rocket
Familiar affections, shaped in time's careworn fingers
Are useful landmarks urging us onward

Serenity reborn with an evening in a hammock hotel
Through the shiftless plains, the bison jungle,
    the untouched solitude
A mirror image of a nomad's toothless tale

To Fleet Street and the Boardwalk Inn
Kittens, kites and mandolin merchants
Butterfly nets and a Bocce race
And a boy with a sackful of yesterdays
As I turn for a second, a startling scene
The best and worst of laughable letterforms
Inconsistently invigorating, shout out my name
Wheels hault—ears engage—body adjusts
And if language could reproduce the experience
I would jot it down in words for you
But the most I can say is a wrinkle in time
Let me gaze through a fundamental keyhole
One that I know I will someday see more clearly
In an instant the disjointed pieces made sense
Happiness became a lost code from the past

Byways were no longer swarming and the air wasn't thin
Afternoons of velvet friendships and flavored teas…
Ordinary days on the lake now a quilted pattern
I could nearly grasp

The rattling, rustling, swaggering streets stood still
At once a brown-eyed,
    winter dressed figure approached me
And as he drew nearer my hobo soul began to sing
    And sing—
        And it sang for an unbroken length

The echo went wildly through a lush backyard
Down into an open woodland and a deep den
Filtered through the Ironwood,
    Sassafras and Chinaberry
Releasing the river elves from their queer slumbers
Following the high-pass,
    Its melody unfroze the Sleeping Giant
From his otherworldly sanctuary on Roseboat pond
Heaven's heartbeat pulsed for that brief second
The gas lanterns flickered, children turned in their beds
A universal pause returned the natural
                        hue of my complexion

With hobo hands, I praised
Again with purpose, again with ease

This ungirded gulf of discovery
A palpable specter—unexpected guest
But one with familiar eyes both unused and unburdened
Massaging the speckled land with seedlings
    —Tiny green gift boxes of revelation

It was yesterday we played hide-and-seek at the
                Callander rooftop garden

    Today I'm counting cobblestones in Marseilles
            Dressed in my favorite striped anorak

Under Innocent Eyes

In those milky white schoolyard days
Past the treetower stairs
I clung to a canvas sack
And stepped in time to mother's high heels
As she walked me to the musty classroom
With the bookshelf corner

Passionate about the reading lounge table
Caped in a raincoat jersey
I was enamoured by the pattering of raindrops
On the hazy classroom window
Reawakening the hunger in my eyes
To let these foggy moments
Chisel out a permanent groove in my shadow

Even now I can summon the smells,
The sentences spoken,
And the facial expressions of those formative years

My nimble toes and impressionable ears
Bounded down the sighing path
A polite smile arose from my cheeks
In those windswept hours by the fence happy squares
Where merry spirits howled and parents watched
As their seedlings blossomed like hot pumpkin pies
Straight out of a breasted mother's love and ingenuity

In her high-backed chair
My crippled teacher wrote
Timeless letterforms on the dry-crackled
Blackboard movie screen
Lollipopped youngsters sat listening
To her enchanted see-saw voice
As it paused on the wood tops of our desks
And crumbled, then died in the linoleum floorlines

We didn't know
The knocking of the wall clock
Grey hairs in our teacher's twisting ringlets
Was our future
The deathly destiny of our youthful yearnings
But we were the new fresh pepper
Salt under every footstep planted
Recent extensions of the population
Capped and bedded, snappy and daring

We saw the pinwheel stirring
The frenzied giraffe stampede
From our encased world of wastepaper blowguns
And elastic loop guns
Aimed strategically at the teacher's seat

Our chrome pinballs clinked through metal pegs
We pulled back the shooters to watch
As together we scored wooden lanes
Knee socks, fighter jets and library trips

Kept us engrossed until I sprang up in bed to view
the timepiece:
6:02 on a Friday
32 years of age

Janulienka

Those sea-green wardrobe eyes
Always youthful in their plea
Look out from a heart so warm
To make sense of what they see

Moon

You sad cyclops eye
Hauntingly hanging in the heavens
Only faint hints of light
Give you away

Heavy stone sphere
Lifelessly lingering above us
As if the anti-hero of earth
You wait and watch

Oh, Nighttime's nanny
Hope of a new day coming
Peering down into the rooms of the children
Lending your peaceful, spellbound sleep

Forest

A green splash stains a clean horizon
Destroying its perfect line
A myriad of umbrella men
Tangled in disguise

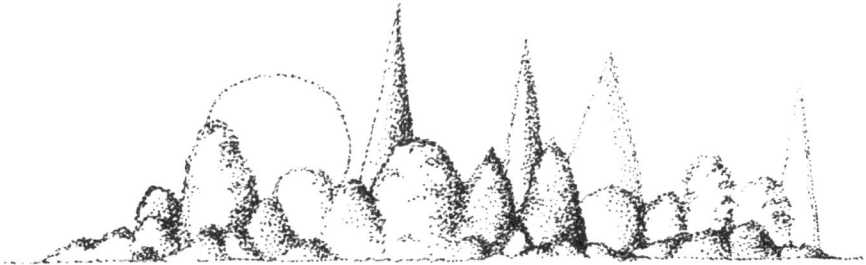

I Remember in Childhood

I remember in childhood, the tea-cosy cookhouse.
There were fresh sweet rolls and puffed delicacies in
the brick baking-chamber. I held my tongue out,
unraveled, pausing to devour the faintest nibble when
Aunt Helen initiated a long drawn-out dialogue on the
art of braiding threads to make baskets and the baleen
used from whales.

It was a sharp and knife-edged existence, growing up
in the French quarter, beside jellyfish quarry. My father
was a deep-seated lover of people. His consistency in
prayer bathed us in an unfathomable grace. Yet the
meager lot in life that we endured spelled out a
suffering unimaginable.

When the drought doubled our foliage decay and the
parched grass became standard, all of my sisters and
myself were out fine-tooth investigating the town
employment books.

At once I chanced upon a dramaturgy plea. A local
theatre troupe wanted a man to look after the stagecraft
duties and wave the curtains in the animated faces of
showgoers when the stilt clappers and the workshop
wagons crept on all threes amid the cast-iron gasolier
entranceway.

Intertwined in the stuffing of my romanticized entrails,
I noted a flutter almost too faint to perceive. This rising
auditorium-destined undulation strengthened slowly
to become a burst of infatuation for that which my soul
thirsted. A charged chortle flung my legsticks into the
air beside my hips and I started to skip crosswise the
breathing footpath. And betwixt the duskfall crescent
torchlight and the meeting house bin, I birthed a
strange song:

Shadow hands and eyedrop tears
Won't stop my casting out my fear
And running, leaping, dusting off these alabaster doves

I see the topmost flags in town
Then rip my heart and throw it down
Recover quickly, paste a thorn beside this crinkled street

Yon and yon, Oh laugh a bit you hazy duck,
You fickle moon
A tuneful thought in falcon treetop glen upon my name

Yon and yon, Oh skip and shiver, lunge forth
Casting out your fear
This nightfall breeze upon my cheeks
Lifts a flavored scent amid the quick unwinding lane

And to the corner theatre company I approached with footsteps thick. Straight in front of me stood a figure on the center stage catwalk. An embellished story served my good purpose on this glorious occasion. So I told my tale.

'Hello sir! How goest this fine evenin' fer ya sir? My name is Kid Moses and in my past I've been hired to shed light on the actors sir, worked the lighting in the theatre house for a night showing few years back on the banks of the turnpike, back in old town!'

The dark figure made a hasty turn toward me and lent a farcical gaze. 'We take people with talent Kid Moses, only the expert types with skills for the asking. But let me show ya round, and we'll let you try your hand in our kind theatre, at least a night and a day, then you're off if we don't like ya.'

I made my name in that theatre hall. Created memories I'll never forget. As the audience looked up, I danced limberly in air and slid the backdrop painting furniture away. My chiaroscuro songs lit up the room in constant intercourse and threw a funny texture 'cross the walls. Manikin marches and sweeping flashes of sanguine personality and kinetic tick tock gravity shows became a regular happening in that brilliant house on the edge of a dumbfounded universe where heaven met my poor boy love.

Picking up my pedal feet and shoving off to my native lagoon where my mother stays in a terraced tower tilting-house, I found myself again, looking up at that schooldays mansion. Twisting, funneling, upward to evaporate in sky swabs, it was that home of homes; oh vacant land you look so lonesome. Yet my mother dwells coldly on; unencumbered by the timid trees; with a confidence of Christ in her bosom nigh.

Opening the aperture hatchway, I climbed into my antique suite and sat upon that chesterfield, breathing. Upon a sigh, I swung my bony hand into a hole-in-the-wall. A deep-seated shelf to feel my scratch pad there.

An empty page—
A canvas blank to steep in cushioned words.

A feather pen with dip-ink jar on tabletop plank for creating the most oblong, wasteful and delicious sentences about apron-theatre and stage technique. I tried to reveal who I was. My hand, the workings of the heart, unfolding words on paper like a puppet muse. I had tasted the musty humor of backstage umbrella people and gleaned from the skill of the two-faced wood buffoon. My encounter was a fanatical craze for a spotlight bird.

An eager and zealous urge for what was birthing
beneath my speed-wings.

Ready to share these thoughts-on-parchment, I flew on
my toes downstairs to the study. Untangling myself like
a vulnerable mass, my eyes struck my mother's eyes. For
a passing moment in time we touched the soul of the
other, but she didn't understand. She couldn't under-
stand. The capability escaped her.

Her experience was other. Locked in a meandering
puzzle that hadn't been where I had been. She hadn't
the network of wires to catch the current of electricity
that had burnt its teethed mark into my essence. To feel
that moment when within, I screamed with unspeak-
able joy at the sight of my own frail limbs crawling
across the dirty stage floor as tears rinsed my arm hair.
As much as she wanted to comprehend who I was, she
didn't know how. Her soul windows showed signs that
she yearned to figure me out. She desired the same
energy for life of which she caught flitting clues from
observing me. Yet she continued licking her own vomit
from her own cage floor because something deep inside
of her didn't register.

I turned and left.

As the shutters drew back, the laughing forest made
me chuckle and the chariot pumpkin treehouse babes
with cuttlefish pigtails spun around. My shaven nostrils
chilled and ready for an evening of pantomime or
show-stopping choreographed whispers. The backs of
the row houses like idle coffin moments weighing heav-
ily on the streetways of fumbling earth. I stretched out
my toes and juggled the hilltops and ruffled the fields
and braided the skyline and wept for the ocean and
tampered with heaven and unlatched my fingers to
topple a rainbow.

Gabriela

Descending ladders spiral
   She dips her gown in zig-zag pools
Misshapen skies bend the light
   And it slides down captive streams
      Into a shapeless den

Her flooded heart
   Enamoured by a celestial gaze
Within the curly tomb of leafy cage
      Rises to catch a star

Legends of infancy
   Kindled under twilight
When the unbuttoned margins of time
      Meet the intimacy of silence

Death's black pearls
   Replace her garland spirit
As lingering echoes of life
   Attempt a final curtsey
      Before dissolving into ribboned sighs

Her brambled bed, a gulley
   Shrouded by broom-covered hill
Its yellow blossoms shade her figure
      And prophesy the morrow

Nowtide, her speechless chamber breathes
   Dawn's faithful warmth excites
Immortal eyes open fresh and free
   And perplexed by the metamorphosis,
      The skeptics of the wood believe